Psalt

MW00627183

and Mary

A Scriptural Rosary according to Psalms and Proverbs

by Christine Haapala
illustrated by Julius Schnorr von Carolsfeld

Suffering Servant Scriptorium
Fairfax, VA
www.sufferingservant.com

Published with Ecclesiastical Permission
Diocese of Arlington
August 12, 2003

Cover design and book layout by Alison Ujueta

ISBN: 978-0-9703996-6-3

Kindle ISBN: 978-0-9840394-2-5

Manufactured in the United States of America

Dedicated to the
Blessed Virgin Mary,
Queen of Prophets

Special thanks to Father Michael Duesterhaus for his spiritual direction and encouragement.

Table of Illustrations

Table of Contents

THE WAYS OF WISDOM
SIR 30:1-2

Psalter of Jesus and Mary

A Scriptural Rosary according to Psalms and Proverbs

DAVID, THE PSALMIST – GIVING THANKS
Ps 92:1-11

The Joyful Mysteries

The Sign of the Cross

The Apostles' Creed

Let me hear sounds of joy and gladness… *Ps 51:10*

Our Father…

The favors of the LORD I will sing forever; / through all generations my mouth shall proclaim your faithfulness. *Ps 89:2*

Hail Mary…

Take courage and be stouthearted, / all you who hope in the LORD. *Ps 31:25*

Hail Mary…

Love the LORD, all you his faithful ones! *Ps 31:24*

Hail Mary… Glory Be… O My Jesus…

The First Joyful Mystery
The Annunciation

Mary said: "I am the servant of the Lord. Let it be done to me as you say." *Lk 1:38*

Our Father...

THE ANNUNCIATION
LK 1:28-33

Happy the man who follows not / the counsel of the wicked / Nor walks in the way of sinners... / But delights in the law of the LORD / and meditates on his law day and night. *Ps 1:1-2*

Hail Mary...

I will proclaim the decree of the LORD: / The LORD said to me, "You are my son; / this day I have begotten you…" *Ps 2:7*

Hail Mary…

But you, O LORD, are my shield … / When I call out to the LORD, / he answers me from his holy mountain. *Ps 3:4-5*

Hail Mary…

Know that the LORD does wonders for his faithful one … / You put gladness into my heart… *Ps 4:4,8*

Hail Mary…

But I, because of your abundant kindness, / will enter your house; / I will worship at your holy temple… *Ps 5:8*

Hail Mary…

The LORD has heard my plea; / the LORD has accepted my prayer. *Ps 6:10*

Hail Mary…

I will give thanks to the LORD for his justice, / and sing praise to the name of the LORD Most High. *Ps 7:18*

Hail Mary…

ABRAHAM RECEIVES GOD'S PROMISE OF A SON
GN 18:1-10

When I behold your heavens, the work of your fingers ... / What is man that you should be mindful of him; / or the son of man that you should care for him? *Ps 8:4-5*

Hail Mary...

I will give thanks to you, O LORD, with all my heart; / I will declare all your wondrous deeds. *Ps 9:2*

Hail Mary...

His ways are secure at all times... *Ps 10:5*

Hail Mary... Glory Be... O My Jesus...

The Second Joyful Mystery
The Visitation

Elizabeth was filled with the Holy Spirit and cried out in a loud voice: "Blest are you among women and blest is the fruit of your womb." *Lk 1:41-42*

Our Father...

THE BIRTH OF JOHN
LK 1:57-66

In the LORD I take refuge... / "Flee to the mountain like a bird! / ... The LORD is in his holy temple." *Ps 11:1,4*

Hail Mary...

"I will grant safety to him who longs for it." / The promises of the LORD are sure... / You, O LORD, will keep us / and preserve us always from this generation. *Ps 12:6-8*

Hail Mary...

Let my heart rejoice in your salvation; / let me sing of the LORD, "He has been good to me." *Ps 13:6*

Hail Mary...

The LORD looks down from heaven upon the children of men, / to see if there be one who is wise and seeks God. ... / Oh, that out of Zion would come the salvation of Israel! *Ps 14:2,7*

Hail Mary...

Who shall dwell on your holy mountain? / He who walks blamelessly and does justice; / who thinks the truth in his heart. *Ps 15:1-2*

Hail Mary...

Therefore my heart is glad and my soul rejoices ... / You will show me the path to life, / fullness of joys in your presence, / the delights at your right hand forever. *Ps 16:9,11*

Hail Mary...

Hannah's Prayer
1Sm 1:9-18

My steps have been steadfast in your paths, / my feet have not faltered. *Ps 17:5*

Hail Mary...

The LORD rewarded me according to my justice... *Ps 18:21*

Hail Mary...

The heavens declare the glory of God, / and the firmament proclaims his handiwork. *Ps 19:2*

Hail Mary...

May he grant you what is in your heart / and fulfill your every plan. *Ps 20:5*

Hail Mary... Glory Be... O My Jesus...

The Third Joyful Mystery
The Nativity

This day in David's city a savior has been born to you, the Messiah and Lord. *Lk 2:11*

Our Father...

THE STAR IN THE EAST SHINES ON THE INFANT JESUS
MT 2:9-12

For you welcomed him with goodly blessings, / you placed on his head a crown of pure gold. / He asked life of you: ... / For you made him a blessing forever; / you gladdened him with the joy of your presence. *Ps 21:4-5,7*

Hail Mary...

To you I was committed at birth, / From my mother's womb you are my God. *Ps 22:11*

Hail Mary...

The LORD is my shepherd ... / Only goodness and kindness follow me / all the days of my life; / And I shall dwell in the house of the LORD / for years to come. *Ps 23:1,6*

Hail Mary...

Who is this king of glory? / The LORD of hosts; he is the king of glory. *Ps 24:10*

Hail Mary...

To you I lift up my soul, O LORD, my God. / In you I trust ... / No one who waits for you shall be put to shame. *Ps 25:1-3*

Hail Mary...

O LORD, I love the house in which you dwell, / the tenting-place of your glory. *Ps 26:8*

Hail Mary...

The LORD is my light and my salvation ... / One thing I ask of the LORD; / this I seek: / To dwell in the house of the LORD / all the days of my life, / That I may gaze on the loveliness of the LORD... *Ps 27:1,4*

Hail Mary...

RUTH TRAVELS WITH NAOMI TO BETHLEHEM
RUTH 1:11,14-19

[M]y heart exults, and with my song I give him thanks. *Ps 28:7*

Hail Mary...

Give to the LORD glory and praise, / Give to the LORD the glory due his name; / adore the Lord in holy attire. *Ps 29:1-2*

Hail Mary...

"What gain would there be from my lifeblood, / from my going down into the grave?" *Ps 30:10*

Hail Mary... Glory Be... O My Jesus...

The Fourth Joyful Mystery
The Presentation of Jesus in the Temple

Simeon blessed them and said to Mary his mother: "This child is destined to be the downfall and the rise of many in Israel … you yourself shall be pierced with a sword…" *Lk 2:34*

Our Father…

THE INFANT JESUS IN THE TEMPLE
LK 2:29-32

Into your hands I commend my spirit; / you will redeem me, O LORD, O faithful God. *Ps 31:6*

Hail Mary…

I will instruct you and show you the way you should walk; / I will counsel you, keeping my eye on you. *Ps 32:8*

Hail Mary...

May your kindness, O LORD, be upon us / who have put our hope in you. *Ps 33:22*

Hail Mary...

He watches over all his bones; / not one of them shall be broken. *Ps 34:21*

Hail Mary...

"I am your salvation." *Ps 35:3*

Hail Mary...

For with you is the fountain of life, / and in your light we see light. *Ps 36:10*

Hail Mary...

Commit to the LORD your way; / trust in him and he will act. *Ps 37:5*

Hail Mary...

O LORD, all my desire is before you... *Ps 38:10*

Hail Mary...

SOLOMON BUILDS THE TEMPLE
1KGS 6:11-14

Let me know, O LORD, my end / and what is the
number of my days… *Ps 39:5*

Hail Mary…

And he put a new song into my mouth, / a hymn
to our God. / Many shall look on in awe / and
trust in the LORD. *Ps 40:4*

Hail Mary… Glory Be… O My Jesus…

The Fifth Joyful Mystery
The Finding of Jesus in the Temple

He said to them: "Why did you search for me? Did you not know I had to be in my Father's house?" *Lk 2:49*

Our Father...

THE BOY JESUS IN THE TEMPLE
LK 2:46-52

[L]et me stand before you forever. *Ps 41:13*

Hail Mary...

[M]y soul longs for you, O God. *Ps 42:2*

Hail Mary...

Then will I go in to the altar of God, / the God of my gladness and joy... *Ps 43:4*

Hail Mary...

In God we gloried day by day; / your name we praised always. *Ps 44:9*

Hail Mary...

I will make your name memorable through all generations; / therefore shall nations praise you forever and ever. *Ps 45:18*

Hail Mary...

Come! [B]ehold the deeds of the LORD, / the astounding things he has wrought on earth. *Ps 46:9*

Hail Mary...

He chooses for us our inheritance, / the glory of Jacob, whom he loves. *Ps 47:5*

Hail Mary...

They also see, and at once are stunned ... / O God, we ponder your kindness within your temple. *Ps 48:6,10*

Hail Mary...

THE FOUNDATION OF THE TEMPLE IS LAID
EZRA 3:10-13

My mouth shall speak wisdom; / prudence shall be the utterance of my heart. *Ps 49:4*

Hail Mary...

"Gather my faithful ones before me ... / Hear, my people, and I will speak..." *Ps 50:5,7*

Hail Mary... Glory Be... O My Jesus...

Hail Holy Queen...

DAVID, THE PSALMIST – REPENTANT
Ps 51:3-11

The Luminous Mysteries

The Sign of the Cross

The Apostles' Creed

The teaching of the wise is a fountain of life … A glad heart lights up the face… *Prv 13:14; Prv 15:13*

Our Father…

Incline your ear, and hear my words, / … That your trust may be in the LORD…. *Prv 22:17,19*

Hail Mary…

The hope of the just brings them joy… *Prv 10:28*

Hail Mary…

"Those who love me I also love, / and those who seek me find me." *Prv 8:17*

Hail Mary… Glory Be… O My Jesus…

The First Luminous Mystery
The Baptism of Jesus

Zechariah his father, filled with the Holy Spirit, uttered this prophesy: … "And you, O child, shall be called / prophet of the Most High; / For you shall go before the Lord / to prepare straight paths for him." … After Jesus was baptized … a voice from the heavens said, "This is my beloved Son." *Lk 1:67,7; Mt 3:16-17*

Our Father…

THE BAPTISM OF JESUS
MT 3:13-37

The father of a just man will exult with glee; / he who begets a wise son will have joy in him. *Prv 23:24*

Hail Mary...

What, my son, my first born! / what, O son of my womb; / what, O son of my vows! *Prv 31:2*

Hail Mary...

[T]he glory of children is their parentage. *Prv 17:6*

Hail Mary...

My son, if you receive my words / and treasure my commands, / ... Then will you understand the fear of the LORD; / the knowledge of God you will find... *Prv 2:1,5*

Hail Mary...

Lo! I will pour out to you my spirit, / I will acquaint you with my words. *Prv 1:23*

Hail Mary...

The words from a man's mouth are deep waters, / but the source of wisdom is a flowing brook. *Prv 18:4*

Hail Mary...

THE THIRD DAY OF CREATION
GN 1:9-13

Trust in the LORD with all your heart, / ... In all your ways be mindful of him, / and he will make straight your paths. *Prv 3:5-6*

Hail Mary...

Wisdom cries aloud in the street, / in the open squares she raises her voice; / Down the crowded ways she calls out, / at the city gates she utters her words... *Prv 1:20-21*

Hail Mary...

From the fruit of his words a man has his fill of good things, / and the work of his hands comes back to reward him. *Prv 12:14*

Hail Mary...

Walk with wise men and you will become wise... *Prv 13:20*

Hail Mary... Glory Be... O My Jesus...

The Second Luminous Mystery
The Wedding at Cana

[T]here was a wedding at Cana in Galilee, and the mother of Jesus was there. … [T]he wine ran out. … His mother instructed those waiting on table, "Do whatever he tells you." … Jesus performed this first of his signs at Cana. *Jn 2:1,3,5,11*

Our Father…

THE MARRIAGE FEAST IN CANA
JN 2:1-11

Home and possessions are an inheritance from parents, / but a prudent wife is from the LORD. *Prv 19:14*

Hail Mary…

He who finds a wife finds happiness; / it is a favor he receives from the LORD. *Prv 18:22*

Hail Mary...

When one finds a worthy wife, / her value is far beyond pearls. / Her husband, entrusting his heart to her, / has an unfailing prize. *Prv 31:10-11*

Hail Mary...

The LORD is far from the wicked, / but the prayer of the just he hears. *Prv 15:29*

Hail Mary...

The desire of the just ends only in good... *Prv 11:23*

Hail Mary...

Let your father and mother have joy; / let her who bore you exult. *Prv 23:25*

Hail Mary...

Refuse no one the good on which he has a claim / when it is in your power to do it for him. *Prv 3:27*

Hail Mary...

[H]appy is he who is kind to the poor! *Prv 14:21*

Hail Mary...

JACOB AND RACHEL AT THE WELL
GN 29:1-12

Honor the LORD with your wealth, / with first fruits of all your produce; / Then will your barns be filled with grain, / with new wine your vats will overflow. *Prv 3:9-10*

Hail Mary...

Come, eat of my food, / and drink of the wine I have mixed! / Forsake foolishness that you may live; / advance in the way of understanding. *Prv 9:5-6*

Hail Mary... Glory Be... O My Jesus...

The Third Luminous Mystery
The Proclamation of the Kingdom

Jesus said … "I have not come to invite the self-righteous to change of heart, but sinners." … [H]e went up on the mountainside. … [H]e began to teach them: … "Blest are the single-hearted / for they shall see God." *Lk 5:31-32, Mt 5:1-2,8*

Our Father…

THE SERMON ON THE MOUNT
MT 5:1-12

Who can say, "I have made my heart clean, / I am cleansed of my sin"? *Prv 20:9*

Hail Mary…

The nether world and the abyss lie open before the LORD; / how much more the hearts of men! *Prv 15:11*

Hail Mary...

Apply your heart to instruction, / and your ears to words of knowledge. *Prv 23:12*

Hail Mary...

[W]alk in the way of good men, / and keep to the paths of the just. / For the upright will dwell in the land, / the honest will remain in it... *Prv 2:20-21*

Hail Mary...

Instruct a wise man, and he becomes still wiser; / teach a just man, and he advances in learning. *Prv 9:9*

Hail Mary...

Survey the path for your feet, / and let all your ways be sure. / Turn neither to right nor to left, / keep your foot far from evil. *Prv 4:26-27*

Hail Mary...

[W]isdom will enter your heart, / knowledge will please your soul, / Discretion will watch over you, / understanding will guard you; / Saving you from the way of evil men... *Prv 2:10-12*

Hail Mary...

ELIJAH REVIVES THE WIDOW'S SON
1KGS 17:17-24

The teaching of the wise is a fountain of life, / that a man may avoid the snares of death. *Prv 13:14*

Hail Mary...

The fear of the LORD is a fountain of life, / that a man may avoid the snares of death. *Prv 14:27*

Hail Mary...

[H]e who confesses and forsakes [his sins] obtains mercy. *Prv 28:13*

Hail Mary... Glory Be... O My Jesus...

The Fourth Luminous Mystery
The Transfiguration

[Jesus] was transfigured before their eyes. His face became as dazzling as the sun, his clothes as radiant as light. *Mt 17:2*

Our Father...

THE TRANSFIGURATION
MT 17:1-8

From of old I was poured forth, / at the first, before the earth. *Prv 8:23*

Hail Mary...

When there were no depths I was brought forth, /
... Before the mountains were settled into place, /
before the hills, I was brought forth... *Prv 8:24-25*

Hail Mary...

"When he established the heavens I was there,
/ when he marked out the vault over the face
of the deep. / ... I was his delight day by day."
Prv 8:27,30

Hail Mary...

A glad heart lights up the face... *Prv 15:13*

Hail Mary...

[T]he path of the just is like shining light, / that
grows in brilliance till perfect day. *Prv 4:18*

Hail Mary...

The light of the just shines gaily... *Prv 13:9*

Hail Mary...

In the light of the king's countenance is life, / and
his favor is like a rain cloud in spring. *Prv 16:15*

Hail Mary...

The poor and the oppressor have a common
bond: / the Lord gives light to the eyes of both.
Prv 29:13

Hail Mary...

MOSES RECEIVES GOD'S HOLY COMMANDMENTS
EX 20:1-5,7-10; EX 31:18

The beginning of wisdom is the fear of the LORD, / and knowledge of the Holy One is understanding. *Prv 9:10*

Hail Mary...

Be not afraid of sudden terror, / of the ruin of the wicked when it comes; / For the LORD will be your confidence, / and will keep your foot from the snare. *Prv 3:25-26*

Hail Mary... Glory Be... O My Jesus...

The Fifth Luminous Mystery
The Institution of the Eucharist

[T]aking bread and giving thanks, [Jesus] broke it and gave it to them, saying: "This is my body to be given for you. Do this as a remembrance of me. ... This cup is the new covenant in my blood, which will be shed for you." *Lk 22:19-20*

Our Father...

THE HOLY COMMUNION
MT 26:26-28

"Who has gone up to heaven and come down again - / who has cupped the wind in his hands?" *Prv 30:4*

Hail Mary...

"Who has bound up the waters in a cloak - / who has marked out all the ends of the earth?" *Prv 30:4*

Hail Mary...

"What is his name, what is his son's name, / if you know it?" *Prv 30:4*

Hail Mary...

From the fruit of his words a man has his fill of good things, / and the work of his hands comes back to reward him. *Prv 12:14*

Hail Mary...

The path of life leads the prudent man upward, / that he may avoid the nether world below. *Prv 15:24*

Hail Mary...

The just man's recompense leads to life, / the gains of the wicked, to sin. ... In the path of justice there is life... *Prv 10:16, Prv 12:28*

Hail Mary...

Evil men understand nothing of justice, / but those who seek the LORD understand all. *Prv 28:5*

Hail Mary...

The fruit of virtue is a tree of life... *Prv 11:30*

Hail Mary...

THE ORIGIN OF THE PASCHAL LAMB
Ex 12:1,3-8,11-14

God has glory in what he conceals, / kings have glory in what they fathom. / As the heavens in height, and the earth in depth, / the heart of kings is unfathomable. *Prv 25:2-3*

Hail Mary...

If a king is zealous for the rights of the poor, / his throne stands firm forever. *Prv 29:14*

Hail Mary... Glory Be... O My Jesus...

Hail Holy Queen...

DAVID, THE PSALMIST – ASKING FORGIVENESS
Ps 51:12-19

The Sorrowful Mysteries

The Sign of the Cross

The Apostles' Creed

You do see, for you behold misery and sorrow, / taking them in your hands. *Ps 10:14*

Our Father...

O LORD, hear my prayer; / hearken to my pleading in your faithfulness; / in your justice answer me. *Ps 143:1*

Hail Mary...

Why are you so downcast, O my soul? / Why do you sigh within me? / Hope in God! *Ps 42:6*

Hail Mary...

The LORD loves those that hate evil... *Ps 97:10*

Hail Mary... Glory Be... O My Jesus...

The First Sorrowful Mystery
The Agony in the Garden

In his anguish he prayed with all the greater intensity, and his sweat became like drops of blood falling to the ground. *Lk 22:44*

Our Father…

CHRIST'S AGONY IN GETHSEMANE
LK 22:39-44

Have mercy on me, O God, in your goodness; / in the greatness of your compassion… *Ps 51:3*

Hail Mary…

I will thank you always for what you have done, /
and proclaim the goodness of your name / before
your faithful ones. *Ps 52:11*

Hail Mary...

Oh, that out of Zion would come the salvation of
Israel! *Ps 53:7*

Hail Mary...

O God hear my prayer; / hearken to the words of
my mouth. *Ps 54:4*

Hail Mary...

But I will call upon God, / and the LORD will
save me. / In the evening, and at dawn, and at
noon, / I will grieve and moan, / and he will hear
my voice. *Ps 55:17-18*

Hail Mary...

In God in whose promise I glory, / in God I trust
without fear; / what can flesh do against me?
Ps 56:5

Hail Mary...

I call to God the Most High, / to God, my
benefactor. *Ps 57:3*

Hail Mary...

JEREMIAH'S LAMENT
JER 1:1-5,11-12

[H]e shall bathe his feet in the blood... *Ps 58:11*

Hail Mary...

Rescue me from my enemies, O my God; / from my adversaries defend me. *Ps 59:2*

Hail Mary...

Give us aid against the foe ... / Under God we shall do valiantly... *Ps 60:13-14*

Hail Mary... Glory Be... O My Jesus...

The Second Sorrowful Mystery
The Scourging at the Pillar

Pilate's next move was to take Jesus and have him scourged. *Jn 19:1*

Our Father...

THE TRIAL OF CHRIST
MT 26:63-66

Hear, O God, my cry; / listen to my prayer!
Ps 61:2

Hail Mary...

How long will you set upon a man and all together beat him down / as though he were a sagging fence, a battered wall? *Ps 62:4*

Hail Mary...

My soul clings fast to you; / your right hand upholds me / ... They shall be delivered over to the sword... *Ps 63:9,11*

Hail Mary...

Hear, O God, my voice in my lament; / from the dread enemy preserve my life. *Ps 64:2*

Hail Mary...

We are overcome by our sins; / it is you who pardon them. *Ps 65:4*

Hail Mary...

[Y]ou laid a heavy burden on our backs. / You let men ride over our heads; / we went through fire and water... *Ps 66:11-12*

Hail Mary...

So may your way be known upon earth; / among all nations, your salvation. *Ps 67:3*

Hail Mary...

JOB'S ADVERSITY AND FORBEARANCE
JOB 1:13-22

[T]he LORD, my Lord, controls the passageways of death. *Ps 68:21*

Hail Mary...

Rather they put gall in my food, / and in my thirst they gave me vinegar to drink / ... But I am afflicted and in pain; / let your saving help, O God, protect me. *Ps 69:22,30*

Hail Mary...

Let them be put to shame and confounded / who seek my life. *Ps 70:3*

Hail Mary... Glory Be... O My Jesus...

The Third Sorrowful Mystery
The Crowning with Thorns

The soldiers then wove a crown of thorns and fixed it on his head, throwing around his shoulders a cloak of royal purple. *Jn 19:2*

Our Father...

JESUS WITH THE CROWN OF THORNS
MT 27:27-30

In you, O LORD, I take refuge; / let me never be put to shame. *Ps 71:1*

Hail Mary...

O God, with your judgment endow the king, / and with your justice, the king's son... *Ps 72:1*

Hail Mary...

I almost lost my balance; / my feet all but slipped ... / my flesh and my heart waste away. *Ps 73:2,26*

Hail Mary...

[R]emember how the fool blasphemes you day after day. *Ps 74:22*

Hail Mary...

For a cup is in the LORD's hand ... / And he pours out from it. *Ps 75:9*

Hail Mary...

From heaven you made your intervention heard; / the earth feared and was silent / When God arose for judgment, / to save all the afflicted of the earth. *Ps 76:9-10*

Hail Mary...

Aloud to God I cry; / aloud to God to hear me; / on the day of my distress I seek the Lord. *Ps 77:2-3*

Hail Mary...

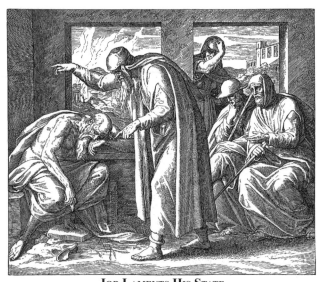

JOB LAMENTS HIS STATE
JOB 19:8-11,25-27

[H]e spared them not from death ... / And he surrendered his strength into captivity, / his glory into the hands of the foe. *Ps 78:50,61*

Hail Mary...

O LORD, how long? *Ps 79:5*

Hail Mary...

May your help be with the man of your right hand, / with the son of man whom you yourself made strong. *Ps 80:18*

Hail Mary... Glory Be... O My Jesus...

The Fourth Sorrowful Mystery
The Carrying of the Cross

Jesus was led away, and carrying the cross by himself, went out to what is called the Place of the Skull. *Jn 19:16b-17*

Our Father...

CHRIST BEARING HIS CROSS
JN 19:17

"I relieved his shoulder of the burden; / his hands were freed ... / In distress you called, and I rescued you." *Ps 81:7-8*

Hail Mary...

"Yet like men you shall die, / and fall like any prince." / Rise, O God. *Ps 82:7-8*

Hail Mary...

For behold, your enemies raise a tumult, / and they who hate you lift up their heads. *Ps 83:3*

Hail Mary...

The LORD withholds no good thing / from those who walk in sincerity. *Ps 84:12*

Hail Mary...

Justice shall walk before him, / and salvation, along the way of his steps. *Ps 85:14*

Hail Mary...

Incline your ear, O LORD; answer me, / for I am afflicted... *Ps 86:1*

Hail Mary...

And of Zion they shall say: / "One and all were born in her; / And he who has established her / is the Most High LORD." *Ps 87:5*

Hail Mary...

THE PROPHET ISAIAH
Is 9:5-6; 53:4-5,12

I am a man without strength / … You have taken my friends away from me… *Ps 88:5,9*

Hail Mary…

Remember how short my life is; / how frail you created all the children of men! *Ps 89:48*

Hail Mary…

You turn man back to dust… *Ps 90:3*

Hail Mary… Glory Be… O My Jesus…

The Fifth Sorrowful Mystery
The Crucifixion

Near the cross of Jesus there stood his mother …
"Now it is finished." Then he bowed his head,
and delivered over his spirit. *Jn 19:25,30*

Our Father…

JESUS DIES ON THE CROSS
JN 19:25-30

I will deliver him and glorify him… *Ps 91:15*

Hail Mary…

It is good … / To proclaim your kindness at dawn / and your faithfulness throughout the night. *Ps 92:2-3*

Hail Mary…

The floods lift up, O LORD, / the floods lift up their voice; / the floods lift up their tumult. *Ps 93:3*

Hail Mary…

[T]hey attack the life of the just / and condemn innocent blood. *Ps 94:21*

Hail Mary…

In his hands are the depths of the earth. *Ps 95:4*

Hail Mary…

Tremble before him, all the earth; / say among the nations: The LORD is king. *Ps 96:9-10*

Hail Mary…

Clouds and darkness are round about him… *Ps 97:2*

Hail Mary…

His right hand has won victory for him, / his holy arm. / The LORD has made his salvation known. *Ps 98:1-2*

Hail Mary…

THE SACRIFICE OF ISAAC
GN 22:2-12

The LORD is king; the peoples tremble; / he is throned upon the cherubim; the earth quakes / … a forgiving God you were to them. *Ps 99:1,8*

Hail Mary…

Know that the LORD is God; / he made us, his we are; / his people, the flock he tends. *Ps 100:3*

Hail Mary… Glory Be… O My Jesus…

Hail Holy Queen…

THE BURIAL OF CHRIST
JN 19:38-42

DAVID, THE PSALMIST – PRAISING THE LORD
Ps 103:1-13,21-22

The Glorious Mysteries

The Sign of the Cross

The Apostles' Creed

O LORD, our Lord, / how glorious is your name over all the earth! ... / Give to the LORD the glory due his name... *Ps 8:2; Ps 29:2*

Our Father...

Mighty are you, O LORD, and your faithfulness surrounds you. *Ps 89:9*

Hail Mary...

And now, for what do I wait, O LORD? / In you is my hope. *Ps 39:8*

Hail Mary...

The LORD keeps all who love him... *Ps 145:20*

Hail Mary... Glory Be... O My Jesus...

The First Glorious Mystery
The Resurrection

Mary Magdalene went to the disciples. "I have seen the Lord!" *Jn 20:18*

Our Father…

THE RISEN CHRIST APPEARS TO MARY MAGDALENE
JN 20:14-17

Of kindness and judgment I will sing; / to you, O LORD, I will sing praise. *Ps 101:1*

Hail Mary…

But you, O LORD, abide forever, / and your name through all generations. / You will arise …
Ps 102:13-14

Hail Mary...

The LORD has established his throne in heaven, / and his kingdom rules over all. *Ps 103:19*

Hail Mary...

O LORD, my God, you are great indeed! / You are clothed with majesty and glory, / robed in light… *Ps 104:1-2*

Hail Mary...

Give thanks to the LORD, invoke his name; / make known among the nations his deeds. *Ps 105:1*

Hail Mary...

Yet he saved them for his name's sake, / to make known his power. *Ps 106:8*

Hail Mary...

Let them give thanks to the LORD for his kindness / and his wondrous deeds to the children of men. *Ps 107:15*

Hail Mary...

The Sabbath
Gn 2:1-4

Be exalted above the heavens, O God; / over all the earth be your glory! *Ps 108:6*

Hail Mary...

I will speak my thanks earnestly to the LORD, / and in the midst of the throng I will praise him... *Ps 109:30*

Hail Mary...

The LORD said to my Lord: "Sit at my right hand..." *Ps 110:1*

Hail Mary... Glory Be... O My Jesus...

The Second Glorious Mystery
The Ascension

He was lifted up before their eyes in a cloud which took him from their sight. *Acts 1:9*

Our Father...

THE ASCENSION OF CHRIST
ACTS 1:9-11

He has made known to his people the power of his works... *Ps 111:6*

Hail Mary...

[H]is horn shall be exalted in glory. *Ps 112:9*

Hail Mary...

Who is like the LORD, our God, who is enthroned on high / and looks upon the heavens and the earth below? *Ps 113:5-6*

Hail Mary...

Before the face of the Lord, tremble, O earth, / before the face of the God of Jacob... *Ps 114:7*

Hail Mary...

Our God is in heaven; / whatever he wills, he does. *Ps 115:3*

Hail Mary...

How shall I make a return to the LORD / for all the good he has done for me? *Ps 116:12*

Hail Mary...

Praise the LORD, all you nations; / glorify him, all you peoples! *Ps 117:1*

Hail Mary...

Open to me the gates of justice; / I will enter them and give thanks to the LORD. *Ps 118:19*

Hail Mary...

I rejoice at your promise... *Ps 119:162*

Hail Mary...

ELIJAH ASCENDS TO HEAVEN
2KGS 2:11-13

All too long have I dwelt / with those who hate peace. *Ps 120:6*

Hail Mary… Glory Be… O My Jesus…

The Third Glorious Mystery
The Descent of the Holy Spirit

Tongues as of fire appeared, which parted and came to rest on each of them. All were filled with the Holy Spirit. *Acts 2:3-4*

Our Father...

THE DESCENT OF THE HOLY GHOST
ACTS 2:1-4

The LORD will guard your coming and your going, / both now and forever. *Ps 121:8*

Hail Mary...

I will say, "Peace be within you!" / Because of the house of the LORD, our God, / I will pray for your good. *Ps 122:8-9*

Hail Mary...

To you I lift up my eyes / who are enthroned in heaven. *Ps 123:1*

Hail Mary...

Our help is in the name of the LORD, / who made heaven and earth. *Ps 124:8*

Hail Mary...

Mountains are round about Jerusalem; / so the LORD is round about his people, / both now and forever. *Ps 125:2*

Hail Mary...

The LORD has done great things for us; / we are glad indeed. *Ps 126:3*

Hail Mary...

Behold, sons are a gift from the LORD; / the fruit of the womb is a reward. *Ps 127:3*

Hail Mary...

THE FIRST DAY OF CREATION
GN 1:1-5

Happy are you who fear the LORD, / who walk in his ways! *Ps 128:1*

Hail Mary...

"The blessing of the LORD be upon you! / We bless you in the name of the LORD!" *Ps 129:8*

Hail Mary...

I trust in the LORD; / my soul trusts in his word. *Ps 130:5*

Hail Mary... Glory Be... O My Jesus...

The Fourth Glorious Mystery
The Assumption of the
Blessed Virgin Mary into Heaven

Then Mary said: ... / "He has deposed the mighty from their thrones / and raised the lowly to high places." *Lk 1:46,52*

Our Father...

MICHAEL AND HIS ANGELS FIGHT THE DRAGON
RV 12:7-12

O LORD, my heart is not proud ... / I busy not myself with great things, / nor with things too sublime for me. *Ps 131:1*

Hail Mary...

In her will I make a horn to sprout for David; / I will place a lamp for my anointed. *Ps 132:17*

Hail Mary...

Behold, how good it is / ... For there the LORD has pronounced his blessing, / life forever. *Ps 133:1,3*

Hail Mary...

Lift up your hands toward the sanctuary, / and bless the LORD. *Ps 134:2*

Hail Mary...

He sent signs and wonders / into your midst... *Ps 135:9*

Hail Mary...

Give thanks to the God of heaven, / for his mercy endures forever. *Ps 136:26*

Hail Mary...

"Sing for us the songs of Zion!" *Ps 137:3*

Hail Mary...

The LORD will complete what he has done for me... *Ps 138:8*

Hail Mary...

JACOB'S DREAM
GN 28:10-17

[Y]ou knit me in my mother's womb. / I give you thanks that I am fearfully, wonderfully made; / wonderful are your works. *Ps 139:13-14*

Hail Mary...

[T]he upright shall dwell in your presence. *Ps 140:14*

Hail Mary... Glory Be... O My Jesus...

The Fifth Glorious Mystery
The Coronation of Mary,
Queen of Heaven and Earth

Then Mary said: … / "For he has looked upon his servant in her lowliness; / all ages to come shall call me blessed." *Lk 1:46,48*

Our Father…

THE NEW HEAVEN AND THE NEW EARTH
Rv 21:1-5

For toward you, O GOD, my Lord, my eyes are turned… *Ps 141:8*

Hail Mary…

Lead me forth … / that I may give thanks to your name. / The just shall gather around me / when you have been good to me. *Ps 142:8*

Hail Mary…

I remember the days of old; / I meditate on all your doings, / the works of your hands I ponder. / I stretch out my hands to you. *Ps 143:5-6*

Hail Mary…

Blessed be the LORD, my rock … / My refuge and fortress, / my stronghold, my deliverer, / My shield, in whom I trust… *Ps 144:1-2*

Hail Mary…

Let them discourse of the glory of your kingdom / and speak of your might, / Making known to men your might / and the glorious splendor of your kingdom. *Ps 145:11-12*

Hail Mary…

The LORD raises up those that were bowed down; / the LORD loves the just. *Ps 146:8*

Hail Mary…

Great is our Lord and mighty in power; / to his wisdom there is no limit. / The LORD sustains the lowly… *Ps 147:5-6*

Hail Mary…

THE FOURTH DAY OF CREATION
GN 1:14-19

Praise the LORD from the heavens / ... Praise him, sun and moon; / praise him, all you shining stars. *Ps 148:1,3*

Hail Mary...

For the LORD loves his people, / and he adorns the lowly with victory. / Let the faithful exult in glory... *Ps 149:4-5*

Hail Mary...

Praise the LORD in his sanctuary, / praise him in the firmament of his strength. / Praise him for his mighty deeds / ... Let everything that has breath / praise the LORD! Alleluia. *Ps 150:1-2,6*

Hail Mary... Glory Be... O My Jesus...

Hail Holy Queen...

THE WORD OF THE LORD TO SAMUEL
1Sm 3:8-13

Author's Note

The praying of the Most Holy Rosary includes both "mental prayer and vocal prayer."[1] Meditation on the mysteries of the Rosary is hard[2] and saying the mantra of Hail Marys can degrade to "mechanical repetition of formulas."[3] Sometimes we get caught up in the chanting of the familiar prayers that our minds wander – to prevent this, a Rosary needs to be prayed in concert with meditation – two things at one time – vocal and mental prayer. "The Rosary calls for a quiet rhythm and a lingering pace ... to meditate on the mysteries of the Lord's life as seen through the eyes of her who was closest to the Lord."[4]

Pope Blessed John Paul II said the Rosary "deserves to be rediscovered. ... Rediscover the Rosary in the light of Scripture."[5] By combining the Sacred Word of God with the prayers of the Rosary we have a special prayer known as a Scriptural Rosary. Pope Paul VI said "prayer should accompany the reading of Sacred Scripture, so that God and man may talk together; for 'we speak to Him when we pray; we hear Him when we read the divine saying.'"[6] Even though we have difficulty understanding and comprehending God's mysterious plan, the Bible meditations allow us to ponder more deeply the mysteries. "Eye has not seen, ear has not heard, / nor has it so much as dawned on man / what God has prepared for those who love him."[7] For "What is unseen is eternal."[8]

A Scriptural Rosary simplifies, yet spiritually edifies,

the meditation process of the praying of the Most Holy Rosary. A Scriptural Rosary is a conversation with God. He speaks to us through His Word and we respond with the Our Father, or the Angelic salutation, the Hail Mary. Sacred Scriptures are added to the praying of the Most Holy Rosary to keep us alert, to help us understand the mysteries, and to converse with God in the presence of His Blessed Mother. "Your prayer is a conversation with God. When you read, God speaks to you; when you pray, you speak to God."[9]

The origins of the Most Holy Rosary date back more than one-half millennium and tradition roots it in the praying of the 150 Psalms. The laity substituted the daily praying of the Psalms with the *Pater Noster* and the *Ave Maria* and counted the prayers on cords of 50 beads. Based on the connection to the Psalms, the Most Holy Rosary has been called the Psalter of Jesus and Mary.[10] St. Augustine said of the Psalms that he heard the "voice of Christ alone and sometimes [the voice] of the Church alone."[11]

A Scriptural Rosary based on the 150 Psalms was written over a decade ago. The selections for the Joyful, Sorrowful and Glorious mysteries from the 150 Psalms first appeared in the author's book <u>From Genesis to Revelation: Seven Scriptural Rosaries</u> as the fourth Scriptural Rosary in the series. For the Joyful, Sorrowful and Glorious mysteries the selections were from the Psalms in order from 1 to 150. Psalms 1 through 10 provided meditations for the First Joyful Mystery, The Annunciation. The meditations continue in order for the other mysteries and concluded with Psalms 141 through 150 for the Fifth Glorious Mystery, The Coronation of Mary, Queen of Heaven and Earth.

More profound than the numerical relationship between the Rosary and the Psalms is the Blessed Virgin Mary would have read and prayed the Psalms with her parents, Sts. Anne and Joachim. Mary would probably have memorized them and "mediate[d] on his law day and night."[12] Much like we read Bible stories to our children, so would Mary's parents have told her stories of her Jewish heritage from scrolls/books we now know as the Old Testament. Similarly, Mary would have shared these same Psalms and stories with her Divine Son Jesus. In quoting St. Augustine, Pope Paul VI wrote "God, the inspirer and author of both Testaments, wisely arranged that the New Testament be hidden in the Old and the Old be made manifest in the New."[13] Christ said to his disciples "everything written about me in the law of Moses and in the prophets and psalms must be fulfilled."[14] One of Christ's seven last words on the cross was from Psalms, "My God, my God, why have you abandoned me?"[15]

For many centuries, the Most Holy Rosary consisted of fifteen decades prayed in three groups of mysteries – the Joyful, Sorrowful, and the Glorious. Pope Blessed John Paul II recommended an additional set of mysteries, the Luminous Mysteries. These

Mysteries of Light "bring out the Christological depth of the Rosary."[16] Pope Blessed John Paul II saw fit to fill in the chronological gap between the Fifth Joyful Mystery with Jesus as a boy of twelve in the temple and the beginning of Jesus' Passion in the Garden of Gethsemane. With the Luminous Mysteries, we now meditate on the significant events of Jesus' public life and ministry.

For some, the addition of the Luminous Mysteries may cause concern because of the departure from the tradition of 500 years of praying the Most Holy Rosary. Rather we should be renewed and energized by the addition of these new Luminous Mysteries, looking forward to a revitalization of the praying of the Most Holy Rosary among the Catholic community. Even more than Catholics, Pope Leo XIII commended the Rosary as a means to "expand the kingdom of Christ" and as "the reconciliation to the Church of nations which have become separated from her."[17]

This pocketsize book includes the Psalms Scriptural Rosary mentioned earlier from <u>From Genesis to Revelation: Seven Scriptural Rosaries</u>. To unveil the new Luminous Mysteries in light of Scripture, we selected meditations from the thirty-one Proverbs, the wise words of Solomon. Each of the twenty mysteries opens with a New Testament passage highlighting one aspect of the mystery followed by praying the Our Father – the prayer Jesus taught us.[18] A short Scripture meditation from either the Psalms or Proverbs introduces each Hail Mary. Each mystery has "suitable icon[s] to portray it."[19] The inspired works from Julius Schnorr von Carolsfeld's Treasury of Bible Illustrations illustrate this book. Each mystery includes two illustrations, one from the Old Testament and one from the New Testament.

These are some examples of the connections between the Old and New Testaments that we have presented through the use of two icons for each mystery of the Rosary.

•Abraham was promised both a son in his old age and also to become the "father of many nations".[20] Israel was promised the Messiah, the Son of God, to save all nations. Mary is "a woman of hope who, like Abraham, accepted God's will … and is a radiant model for those who entrust themselves with all their hearts to the promises of God."[21]

•Hannah, like St. Elizabeth, was old and barren, but they prayed and wept for many years to bear a son, and so they conceived, for "nothing will be impossible for God."[22] They both dedicated their sons, Samuel and St. John the Baptist, to the "LORD as long as he lives."[23]

•Ruth, the great-grandmother of King David, accompanied her mother-in-law back to Bethlehem. Jesus would be born in Bethlehem as Joseph and Mary traveled there during the Roman census. St. Joseph and the Blessed Virgin Mary are of the house of David.

•The "perpetual ordinance"[24] of the Paschal Feast at the time of Moses is the old covenant. The "Lamb of God"[25] institutes the Eucharist as the sacrifice of His body and blood, when he said "This cup is the new covenant in my blood, which will be shed for you."[26]

•The sufferings of Job, lamentations of Jeremiah, and the prophet message of Isaiah's Suffering Servant are fitting Old Testament reflections of the Sorrowful Mysteries where Jesus Christ's "sweat became like drops of bloods"[27] flowing along the Via Dolorosa toward Calvary.

•Just as dramatic as the scene of Elijah ascending to heaven on a fiery chariot, so was Jesus' Ascension. It was a powerful and striking event for the Apostles who were mesmerized and stared into the clouds, until an angel told the apostles that Jesus "would return in the same way as you have seen him going into heaven."[28]

•Jacob dreamed of walking the ladder to heaven. Mary was assumed into heaven, body and soul, and is in the presence of the beatific vision – the Blessed Trinity.[29]

We hope in some small way that this prayer book brings the Most Holy Rosary alive and anew, so that you will "persevere in prayer"[30] and "pray without ceasing."[31] May God bless you and may the mantle of Mary always protect you and your loved ones.

1 St. Louis de Montfort, <u>The Secret of the Rosary</u>, 1st Rose.

2 Montfort, <u>Secret</u>, 43rd Rose.

3 Pope Paul VI, *Marialis Cultus*, Feb, 1974, 47.

4 *Marialis Cultus*, 47.

5 Pope Blessed John Paul II, Apostolic Letter *Rosarium Virginis Mariae,* Oct, 2002, 43.

6 Pope Paul VI, *Dei Verbum*, Nov, 1965, 25.

7 1Cor 2:9.

8 2Cor 4:18.

9 St. Augustine, On Psalm 85.

10 Montfort, <u>Secret</u>, 6th Rose.

11 St. Augustine, On Psalm 59.

12 Ps 1:2.

13 *Dei Verbum*, 16.

14 Lk 24:44.

15 Ps 22:7.

16 *Rosarium Virginis Mariae*, 19.

17 Pope Leo XIII, Adiutricem Populi, Sept, 1895, 4.

18 Mt 6:9-1319 Rosarium Virginis Mariae, 29.

20 Gn 17:16.

21 Pope Blessed John Paul II, *Tertio Millennio Adveniente*, Nov, 1994, 48.

22 Lk 1:37.

23 1Sm 1:11.

24 Ex 12:24.

25 Jn 1:29.

26 Lk 22:20.

27 Lk 22:44.

28 Acts 1:11.

29 Pope Pius XII, *Munificentissimus Deus*, Nov, 1950, 42.

30 Col 4:2.

31 1Thes 5:17

How to Pray the Most Holy Rosary

While holding the Crucifix in the hand, make the *Sign of the Cross* and recite the *Apostles' Creed*. On the first large bead, recite the *Our Father*. On the three small beads recite the *Hail Mary* for an increase in the three theological virtues of faith, hope, and love, next pray the *Glory Be*. Mention each mystery and then recite on the larger bead the *Our Father*. On the decade of ten small beads meditate on the mystery and recite on each bead the Hail Mary. In closing each decade, recite the *Glory Be*, followed by the *O My Jesus* prayer. Repeat this sequence of prayers for five decades. Conclude the Most Holy Rosary by praying the *Hail Holy Queen*.

For many centuries, the Most Holy Rosary was prayed in three sets of mysteries – the Joyful, Sorrowful, and the Glorious. Pope Blessed John Paul II in his Apostolic Letter *Rosarium Virginis Mariae* recommended an additional set of mysteries, the Luminous Mysteries.

While a complete Rosary consists of praying all twenty mysteries, it is more typical of group prayer to only pray five decades at a time. For children or beginners, a five or twenty decade Rosary may be daunting, so begin praying with just a one decade Rosary. While praying include reading of Sacred Scriptures about each mystery to bring the melody of prayer alive with mental pictures of persons, places, and events.

Originally, the Joyful Mysteries were prayed on Monday and Thursday, the Sorrowful Mysteries on Tuesday and Friday, and the Glorious Mysteries on Wednesday, Saturday, and Sunday. With the addition of the Luminous Mysteries, Pope Blessed John Paul II recommended the Joyful Mysteries be prayed on Saturday and the Luminous Mysteries on Thursday.

The Prayers of the Most Holy Rosary

The Apostles' Creed

I believe in God, the Father almighty, Creator of heaven and earth, and in Jesus Christ, his only Son, our Lord, who was conceived by the Holy Spirit, born of the Virgin Mary, suffered under Pontius Pilate, was crucified, died and was buried; he descended into hell; on the third day he rose again from the dead; he ascended into heaven, and is seated at the right hand of God the Father almighty; from there he will come to judge the living and the dead. I believe in the Holy Spirit, the holy catholic Church, the communion of saints, the forgiveness of sins, the resurrection of the body, and life everlasting. Amen.

The Our Father

Our Father, Who art in Heaven, hallowed be Thy Name. Thy kingdom come; Thy will be done on earth as it is in Heaven. Give us this day our daily bread, and forgive us our trespasses, as we forgive those who trespass against us. And lead us not into temptation, but deliver us from evil. Amen.

Hail Mary

Hail Mary, full of grace, the Lord is with thee; blessed art thou among women, and blessed is the Fruit of thy womb, Jesus. Holy Mary, Mother of God, pray for us sinners, now and at the hour of our death. Amen.

Glory Be

Glory be to the Father, and to the Son, and to the Holy Spirit. As it was in the beginning, is now, and ever shall be, world without end. Amen.

The Fatima Prayer

O My Jesus, forgive us our sins; save us from the fires of Hell, lead all souls to Heaven, especially those who are in most need of Thy Mercy.

Hail Holy Queen

Hail, holy Queen, Mother of mercy, our life, our sweetness and our hope. To thee do we cry, poor banished children of Eve! To thee do we send up our sighs, mourning and weeping in this valley of tears. Turn then, most gracious advocate, thine eyes of mercy towards us. And after this, our exile, show unto us the blessed Fruit of thy womb, Jesus. O clement, O loving, O sweet Virgin Mary. Pray for us, O holy Mother of God, that we may be made worthy of the promises of Christ.

Prayer after Most Holy Rosary

O God, whose only begotten Son, by His life, death and resurrection, has purchased for us the rewards of eternal life; grant, we beseech Thee, that, meditating upon these mysteries of the Most Holy Rosary of the Blessed Virgin Mary, we may imitate what they contain and obtain what they promise, through the same Christ our Lord. Amen.

May the divine assistance remain always with us. And may the souls of the faithful departed, through the mercy of God, rest in peace. Amen.

Products from
𝕾uffering 𝕾ervant 𝕾criptorium

Prayer Books for Children of All Ages

<u>Speak, Lord, I am Listening</u> A Rosary Book (2nd Ed. with Luminous Mysteries. Includes Study and Discussion Guide) This prayer book presents the richness of the Sacred Mysteries of the Most Holy Rosary in terms that children can visualize and understand. Gus Muller's watercolors use the full palette of color expression to explore the depths of the agony of Christ crucified and reach the heights of the Blessed Virgin Mary's glorious reign as Queen of Heaven and Earth. Succinct and most apt meditation selections yield a wealth of spiritual insight into the mysterious events of the lives of Jesus and Mary. The Scriptures and watercolor illustrations coupled with the prayers of the Most Holy Rosary provide a rich meditation platform for teaching prayer and devotion to Jesus and Mary.

<u>Follow Me</u> A Stations of the Cross Book. Inspired watercolors and selections of God's Word introduce children to the suffering of our Savior Jesus Christ by walking each step with Him to Calvary. Along with each station is a heroically holy person who epitomized self-sacrifice and was beatified or canonized by Pope Blessed John Paul II.

Prayer Books for Adults and Teenagers

<u>Pearls of Peace: A Rosary Journey through the Holy Land</u> Spiritually walk in Jesus' footsteps by praying the mysteries of the Most Holy Rosary and meditating on the accompanying Holy Land photography. Follow the Holy Family from Bethlehem to Nazareth to Jerusalem. Walk with Jesus, his Blessed Mother, and his disciples to places, such as, Cana, the Sea of Galilee, Mount of Temptation, Mount Tabor, Garden of Gethsemane, Via Dolorosa, and Calvary. In her ninth Scriptural prayer book, Christine Haapala reveals another view of the mysteries of the Most Holy Rosary through meditations from the Gospels and the Epistles of St. Paul. This book is enriched by the stunning photography of Rev. Gary Coulter, Diocese of Lincoln, who led two pilgrimages

to the Holy Land and documented these spirit-filled journeys through photography.

<u>Seraphim and Cherubim: A Scriptural Chaplet of the Holy Angels</u>
Angels have been with us since the beginning in the "Garden of Eden" and will be with us at the "End of Age." This prayer book joins together Sacred Scripture selections with special invocations to our Blessed Mother and the Holy Archangels. This book includes fabulous full-color pictures from the masters, such as, Raphael, Bruegel the Elder, Perugino and many others. It also includes a newly composed Novena of the Holy Angels and the traditional Litany of the Holy Angels. Those who pray without ceasing and ponder the Good News will find this book equally inspiring and encouraging.

<u>In His Presence: Seven Visits to the Blessed Sacrament</u> This meditation book outlines SEVEN VISITS to the Blessed Sacrament. This prayer book can be used in one evening, such as, during the Holy Thursday Seven Church Pilgrimage. It can be used for seven consecutive days for a special prayer request. And, it can be used periodically, whenever you can spend time visiting Jesus in the Blessed Sacrament. Also available in Kindle format.

<u>His Sorrowful Passion</u> This prayer book integrates Sacred Scripture meditations with the prayers of the Chaplet of Divine Mercy. There are two Scriptural Chaplets: one chronicles Jesus' Passion and the other features the Seven Penitential Psalms. The woodcuts of the 15th century Catholic artist, Albrecht Dürer, illustrate this book.

<u>The Suffering Servant's Courage</u> (2nd Ed. with Luminous Mysteries) This prayer book integrates poignant Sacred Scripture verses about courage and fortitude, the prayers of the Most Holy Rosary, and illustrations from the inspired artistry of the 19th century Catholic illustrator Gustave Dóre.

<u>From Genesis to Revelation: Seven Scriptural Rosaries</u> This prayer book is the most thorough and extensive collection of Scriptural Rosaries you will find anywhere. This prayer book goes well beyond the traditional Scriptural Rosary and penetrates the

heart of the meditative spirit of the mysteries. It addresses many dimensions: time, from the Old to the New Testament; authors, from Moses, Isaiah, to the Evangelists; and perspectives, from the purely historical to deeper spiritual and prayerful insights. Those who pray the Rosary and those who read the Bible will equally find this prayer book inspirational.

Recorded Prayers available on CD

<u>The Sanctity of Life Scriptural Rosary</u> (2nd Ed. with Luminous Mysteries) Sacred Scripture selections prayed with the Most Holy Rosary uniquely brings you God's message of the dignity and sanctity of life. The prayers are accompanied by meditative piano music. Four different readers lead you in more than two hours of prayerful meditations. Includes four songs from the composer and soprano Nancy Scimone, winner of the UNITY Awards 2002 Best Sacramental Album of the Year for ORA PRO NOBIS. Includes 16-page book with the complete text of the Sacred Scripture selections. Double CD. CD 1 includes the Joyful and Luminous Mysteries and CD 2 includes the Sorrowful and Glorious Mysteries.

<u>Time for Mercy</u> Composer and singer Nancy Scimone offers you a new, spiritually uplifting Chaplet of Divine Mercy melody. This Scriptural Chaplet of Divine Mercy is based on the Penitential Psalm Scriptural Chaplet of Divine Mercy from the book, <u>His Sorrowful Passion</u>. Brother Leonard Konopka, MIC, prays selections from the Seven Penitential Psalms, while Nancy Scimone's crystal clear soprano voice brings us God's message of Divine Mercy.

Quantity orders of Suffering Servant Scriptorium books or CDs may be purchased for liturgical, educational, or sale promotional use. For discount schedule and further information, please call toll free 888-652-9494 or write to us at:

Suffering Servant Scriptorium
Special Market Department
PO Box 1126
Springfield, VA 22151